park avenue hits trinity river
bottom in a fresh 21st century
as told to bees roaming among
evergreens of a northwest america

3X3 X3

some or cats

s'plains

how's

IT

bEES

Published at http://lulu.com

See the author spotlight:
http://www.lulu.com/spotlight/besottedchild

3 x **3** x 3, or,
some **cats s'plains** how's IT *bees*

CONTENTS

FOURTEEN STAGES IN ~EUROPEAN~ DIVERGINITY

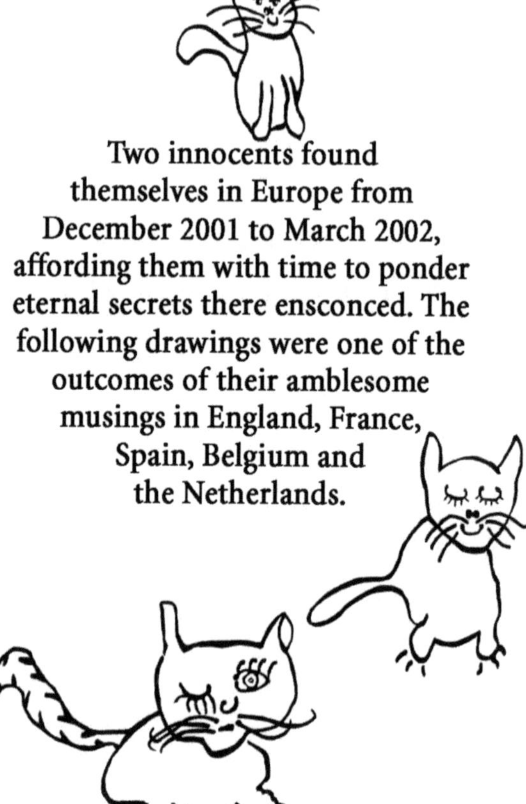

Two innocents found themselves in Europe from December 2001 to March 2002, affording them with time to ponder eternal secrets there ensconced. The following drawings were one of the outcomes of their amblesome musings in England, France, Spain, Belgium and the Netherlands.

Fourteen

The nature of things is

contentment.

Fourteen

Genie of Locale

Thirteen

Who has an idea?

Thirteen

Ideas Come And Go

Twelve

Dead Serious

Suspicious Levitating

Twelve

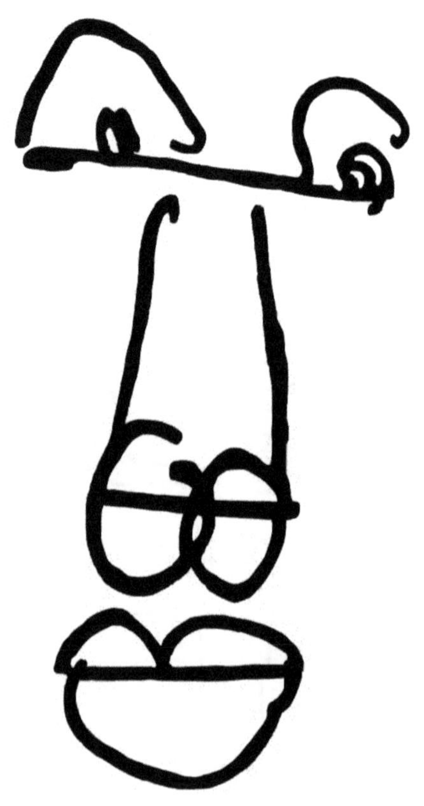

Sirius Inspectus

Eleven

Europa on any ol' day

Eleven

Euphonium

Ten

Bikes and food

Ten

Averse, Universe, Inverse

Nine

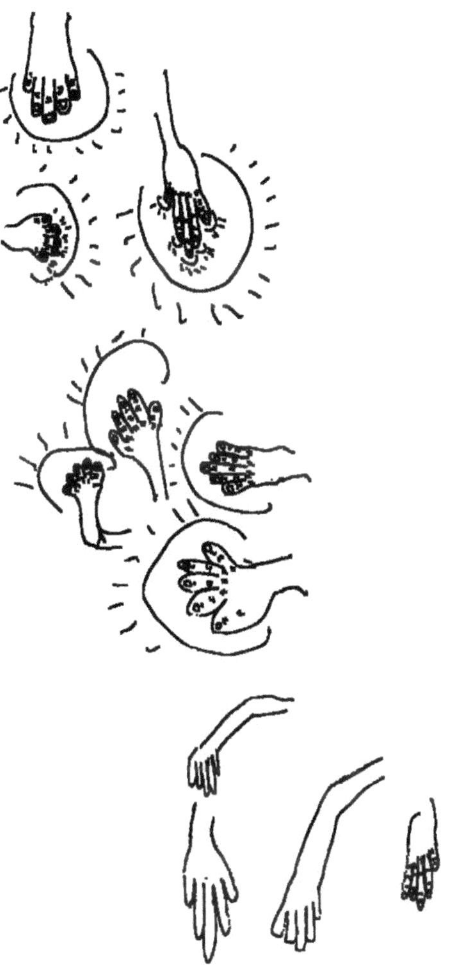

Nine

Don't look past the banks!

Eight

Labyrinth

Eight

Bank it up, you'll be fine.

Seven

Mister A. Gnome, Our Host

Seven

First things first, but which to choose?

Six

Europa has a phone.

Six

Steward recommends *reserve'*

Five

Temptations, many

Five

So much to do

Four

Markets all seemed the same

Four

Glad recommendation to stay

Three

The plan rules.

Three

Just a ball of yarn

(Ne jamais s'affoler, ma petite.)*

Two

Sparkly again

Two

Devotional gazing

One

Believing is acting.

Zero

You get what you see.

BEGINNERS' EUPHONIE STILL REMEMBERED

dog marriage

One a white dwarf yorki
Serious on life,
Other the mastiff believer
Not dreading strife.

Together shimmering
Protection, ripely
Glimmering there, awaiting
Deeply all here.

Road was calling, but that meant a set of wheels. At one point the man said: "This number has little in the way of shocks and doesn't cost all that much either."

It was cash down and off we went.

"Gotta sing a song,
whistle for a train,
watch for it in movies,
start it all again."

some ice cream evening (simply deja moo)

Cold and slippery and soft and wet...
My ice cream dreams I use to vet
Thoughts' coming time. I know it's a bust
But oh, those ice cream dreams
Of which I lust...

Ice cream, yeah, I hear the smooth
Moving inside my mouth's groove,
Sure to lay the land of my soon
To being more real than some
Moon shadow's bloom.

So again to bust I lurch away,
Cradling a blossom to pay
Respect for coming delights
Benighted but not forgot,
Just more real than thought.

on river's edge

High minded again I think of you. No don't
Think me foolish. I know. So very much
Won't go with me in love to your door step,
Over which I've kept our lives in vigil
Civil like a cat awaiting God's fast step.
Vigil, a God sent thing I've liked to you alone,
But with certain doubt, as certain as a wind
In river's waves, cresting most lovely on
Whether it would or would not in the moment
Give so much as a dam cast upon other
Vainly seeking approval from no one but you.
Not that I would play the fool but
That you would me be your partner.

music professor

Major to minor said in
Interval where perfect led,
"Things are more than what they seem
Even when all seems well,
As all who learn studying means
Always adjusting tell."

FELIS SYLPHID SILVESTRIS

Golden eyed Jasper
Said it's a breeze,
Hip bone to thigh
Connects like I to me,
Though blind going this
As it seems,
All come to know
There is sky over the trees.

Kids nowadays... I was on the bus around Halloween and overheard a little one ask her mother if zombies were afraid of their victims, and I chuckled. Mother noticed and winked at me, explaining that they'd bought a zombie costume the night before for the third grade party at school. Smiling at the girl I said:

First bite! Ask questions later.

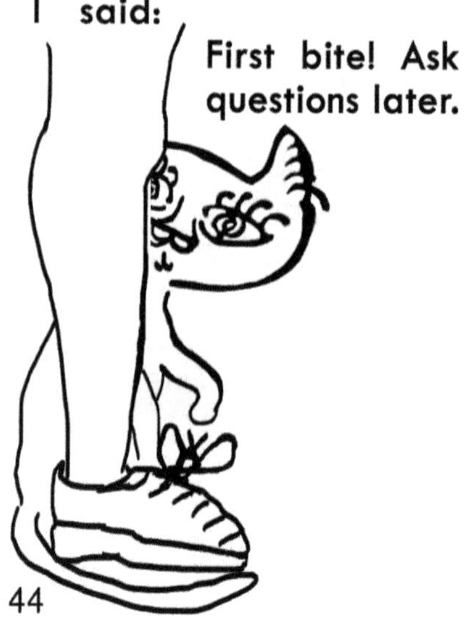

Genie of Locale

You remembered me though
I forgot completely
Where I was, had never
Known what alone meant
Till you told me where
I'd been, showed me a side
That was dark. A spark went
Loving to the place unseen.
Shown what's not sensible
It made clear what is.
Together then we go forgetting
Loving that is without name.

content with things

collect you those numbers,
they are an egg about to happen,
not the content, no, though
making by reason possible what is
lighting a way that's not,
possible being all then content,
what's not merely necessary shell
collecting you; those numbers
go then to what is happening
always by reason enough to be

rain

At strength only
In a certain speed
Under particular light
Below radar
Out of sight
Over all knowing
Comes it flowing for you.

Through sound
Off water
Away from bitter reflection
Beyond rainbow time
Viewing what's not seen
Saying how ever it will be.

Arriving speaking
You, hear for nought
Power we were thinking
Remembering pleased what's bought
Lying near though able.

When comes to now
Beautifully as you go, proud
Dutifully cheering, ways on
Forever, because it's our gold.

Sing I of coming
Hearing what's before
Forgiving one name raining.

Wet, fell I here for
You dear one, none else.

Know us this, eye of storm.

beautiful sunday's forerunner

Like salamanders out of water
Fire without its pith
Into the way of harm we go
It is here begins our bliss

Sorry, no sinking possible
Truth no fence contains
Our way here unstoppable
Again countenancing that's plain

Pan du perdu we will share there
Just for two, one cannot explain
Go figure, if you've a will to
Home then we go to the same

You came to planet Earth—
'Tis extraterrestrial from your birth.
Though alien all can seem
It's the same as where you've been.
That's why you define on Earth
What it is that is of worth.

day's return

Instinct stands
But love defeats right there,
Unless it ends.

I do not know,
Sure as I am of a living smile.
Smiling, you

Assure me. So
To instinct I give love, giving instinct
A free hand.

Freedom, the thing
I know, will I hope defeat love's mishaps,
As jealous guard

Of love's gate.
Leave it time. It may love
In return.

sky's velocity

No acceleration without angularity is what the professor said in class. I might have the wording off a bit, but it's very common knowledge. Velocity alone is not angular relative to known perspectives necessarily, but acceleration is a change in angular momentum relative to all known perspectives. "This is a secret of the weather wherever you happen to be," he said, then advised all in class to in no way allow ourselves to go beneath the sky without . . . our trusty umbrella.

Work itself will energize if you can let it, but requires love under the right conditions, that clear benefits accrue from interests paid. Here, love might be a stealthy behavior, something akin to semaphore between benighted ships during the weather vessels fear to run aground in, or it could be those very good intentions expressed leading to a hell where devil finds himself in service to the Lord. Work makes clear who loves and who will be loved if you can let it.

Euphonie

In the dusty back streets of ol' Tejas where I grew up I heard once a humble cowhand say to his compadre while shoveling out a stable: Jake, bow down 'r bow doin' 'r bend it over 'r bend overn it 'r supplecate ya se'f 'r Sybilatey 'r do whadivver ya gotta do, dammit, but Jesus All'a Christ... GO FER THE MONEY!

Though not yet in grade
school, this I remember.

room in a kiss

There's room in a kiss for impossible I heard.
In your case this is wrong as possible's absurd
Itself, as attested by the soul you wear outside
Like a wedding dress for everyday. Then
There's that honesty, which is taken for an act
In so far as to do so allows response far from tact.
You don't worry though, while, impossibly,
World passes you by, refuting your gentle name.
Kiss as kiss can, I say, I believe you'll rise
As the occasion calls for, impossible decides
Lovingly then whether to show its face again.

If I don't believe in myself first thing in the morning, I don't get to see tomorrow, but, if there's no tomorrow been scheduled then I just take the day off.

moment

Being in the moment
Falling out of time
Wish those eyes were flirting
Better not look at mine
We'll act just like normal
You'll be the one for me
I'll stay not from conforming
Too much to our history
Thus I pray so simply
Here too we sing some songs
Dancing and romancing
All the live long calm
Say we what's important
Only say we when it's caught
This is how we'll do it
It's just the way we're taught

Our server knew that smile. "There's a Texas smile," she said all business like, winking, as she asked mother if she cared for more mustard on that sandwich.

wot noticed

A red door is a fence
On which I've sat
Hoping for the best
Until I put my feet
On the ground, then
Moved on, only to see
That door at a distance
Is black, the boss there
In it's middle I polished
Bright is barely now
Noticeable at all.

S. S. Enterprise, a Radio Flyer, and Rosebud share this quality: capacity to carry you someplace different.

Remembered

In the halls of Babylon
I as a child saw one
As big as a mountain
Speak so well I lost myself;
Was orphaned for awhile.
Babel then became my home...
Was it there I learned to weep,
To roam about, to call for
Help? Then one found me,
Carried me hither,
Thither did I laugh.
Learned I of song, I danced.
So came I to speak as well
As the mountains in my youth.
Now I live in Babylon, know
That you may call when here,
Going our ways when time comes...
Goes life such, yes, good goes life.

A mole I am, I found a gem
Digging as I was, just then.
The gem it was so polished bright
It bade me there to seek the light
And so I did and left it where
Atop the ground it felt the air.
The open air from up the sea,
Mountain winds too, down valleys.
Still go I to see the gem,
If it lies where I placed it then.
I wish somehow it would go away
For it draws me into light of day.
Learned I of value, it is true,
Which is why I tell it you.

catis non gratis

He was all the hard up her good luck could take.

Heard on the back streets of old Seattle: Cross dressing is no lark.

Beginners'

The moon, they say, reflects sun,
I say the stars it reflects as well.
It can be heard to murmur, new,
The thoughts of untold realms.
You, I say reflect the stars,
The sun and all that's good,
One to whom I devote this life
Thus all time here has stood.

Euphonie

Yarn made of string in theory complete
So that if all the right choices made
In time with now make replete
That universal esteem our guarantor
Pays out, like a cat with a ball
Playing, our choices make all happen.

Remember!

***Never lose it,** my little one!

TO

A SUMMER

in ***SEATTLE***

FROM

A WINTER

in ***BARCELONA***

There is a process.
The process is good.
Good.

the beginning

This is a house,
You've been invited,
Enter, be seated, be glad
The meal, it is from locale, farmed,
Woods and lakes and sea
Here prepared as best can be
From source just to feed
Good guests that come.
Please, be kind, be prepared,
Enjoyment, yours, all like
Best. Old wines and legend
Withstanding time's ill tests
Make good here the evening,
Entertaining honored guests.

It tooks a long time learnings to see withsout spectacuhlz fore I'z gotz a realz benefit fromz them.

Hanging in a shadow well
Past fallow years of contemplation
Merely like a picture on the wall
I seem to you imperfect
Toiling in the circuit
Of our love one hundredth time
Breath coming so fine
A reminder that tomorrow
Surrender what we will
Finds us once again our best.
Most sure luxuriance is not
De facto prurience in shame,
It's just the same as now;
You well grown, bolder,
Folding growth as perfect
As any in the circuit
True as love ever was.

hello sky

Don't rush the river,
It sweeps you where it does,
Silence will then tell
...
Just what is above.

heard on the grapevine

Maybe high, maybe low,
Shy or daft, I do not know
Maybe depressed but even so
Only perfection does the job
If the goal's to get demobbed.

If it doesn't make scents, does it
Make sounds? And of touch,
Is it round or square, a bush
Or tree, what's it then
To you and me? Well, friend,
What we know cannot hurt us
If we go out our way in sun
Shining down or darkest day
Because there's work to do
Along with play and loving
Confidence as economy to stay.

... doubt's a river
there let's baptize,
wash away forever what's
untrue, then with sighs,
we'll turn away,
make for the bank
and as on any day
enter the rank and file
of all that is so,
so said, so do,
so life, it goes.

the plan

Odd is just doing something
seen backways round, so
since odd's in viewing one
must be there on ground
to do what's done and so
doing it will be learnt how
fun odd living is, while
doing one's best for now.

time to study

They do a lot of things hard to notice so that's why that safety net thing's up there, but me, I don't pay 'em no never mind on account of I got other stuff a doing.

Gentle staring spirit
Hiding in the grass
Residing in a life
Through which all will pass
That is the good of moments
Felt and known most well,
Gentle staring spirit
Love may let you tell.

Modern world, it has you
Dancing and too, saying grace,
Letting us know how you choose
Is as much a part of the race
As how fast held a house is
Which love does make its shell,
Gentle staring spirit
Let strength that fear dispel.

friends discovered

Life's so full of wonder
But don't let me blunder
Unbidden into yours
Sure as I am it is there
For that time is all yours
Which is to be taken where
When meeting this, the treat
Done like it's common,
Hidden in each moment
Could convince you you're fine.

You're the ink, I the hand
Spelling names you've given.
You think, I cram thoughts of you
Living into eternity.
Glove upon your thoughts, I
Serve only you. Given to concord
Thus we insure what's true.

on the road

Welcome you in your skin,
Perfecting ways to be tried again,
As though they weren't until you came
Succeeding well, just in time
To welcome all, yes, even crying,
Always welcome, so the same
Now and again is good in time.

the next leg

This book, it writes itself, you see
Writing as it's read, so be
Calm and turn the pages while
This train passes all the stages here
On this track to where you're going
To, in the end, just so you be there
Leaving the book here open and on
One page you've been of fond
While stepping off and on the stage
Terminal, the platform for your next
Germinal quest in life, this life
Given you, so another lifts this book.

'happy family'

Imagine that train,
Locomotive of matrimony,
Its fuel being economy
Each day. Passengers are love,
The cars pregnancy,
Children, family; and in the caboose
There's friends for life.
Imagine running for it,
Arranging so it's always nigh,
That track especially important...
Only you must try.
Imagine... this just happens,
So all is orderly,
Well thought out, un-dramatic
But perfect always.

We're Waiting

Let's discuss your paper legs,
the walking you do in books.
This cash paid for those looks
we who abide will not brook.
You will persist, yes we know,
it is so tiring, leaves us cold.
What is it seen inspires you so?
Here we stay, we watch you grow.
It's work you do on those paper legs,
busy always as of old
While we go on living, here
remaining still, waiting to be told
This is next or that is good,
so it goes in all books sold,
Smiles coming down to us
as you fuss and turn the page.
Do you care to fool us that
it's the books have made you brave?
Feel we sure as any page
acquiring looks so thoroughly strange
Fine goes all this very day,
for you, well read, make us happy.

later, sounding again

Let's get around to it,
Make four angles in a pie,
Custom is you blew it,
We'll submit so (just with sighs),
Come again, explain you longing,
Define what's out in the rain,
Smirking as if defrauding
A life not worth the pain.
Then, when time is over
Though deceiving is our pleasure
In a life so full of chores,
Outside wet again we here
Demonstrate what is so, very
Depending and smirk, eyes
Deflected to a curve upon that
Nearness, ah yes, it's but an angle
We'll leave, shutting that door.

to the train, again

Oeuf plat fromage jambon,
Eggs mollet to we when no bone,
Well reminding how we'll go
If we're so lucky to. Day being so
Is night's preternal shadow
Ever soft, and warm then gather
Here the crew to form
Our first ever perfect voyage.

Confidence men, or Federates
Clamber upon the platform here
Sounds of doing, smells a showing
Leading thoughts onto the stage
With mail trucks, vans,
Men, women, ah yes, could be
Gendarmes too, a boy
And his dog, or girl with parasol
Granny with kid, those
Business people truing the lid
On what's so serious, hep to it
Delirious of profit lines,
Oh! Sex does sell, thank God
For that, a glorious day for
More noise, please! Confident
In the sneeze that surrenders
Winking to commend the plan
This time. Taking, giving, click
Clack being, all routes on
Tracks to stay.

toward the chunnel

It was tomorrow yesterday,
Still we won't get there today
Yet... just stop
Asking, so we can make this be
Where we're going.

That road to somewhere else
Starts here
Train of thought stepping
Off there
Leading us out old roads
Or new
Bringing where your thoughts
Go too
Sounding times to be told of
On good
Thoughts, blessing as foretold.

Like a map of foreign terrain
A guidebook for the future, simply
Entertainment across moments
To be endured, enjoyed
Better than otherwise,
You're here always friend,
Hand proffering abundance
Slaking my abhorred absent
Minded habitual love. It
Seeking still a better way finds
All is as it should be, perfect
In you, in me, in moving
To preserve that read by God
Living as God will, willing
Us to be right here always
Entertaining plans we've liked.

weather on the sound

We are of this, you see
You hear, you cannot tear yourself away
Though you would. Thunder
Stood and you did not notice it was
In the way so came on
Claiming time enough to lead into
Ways fine, thought mindful
By some, mere chatter by others, know how
Said thoughtless of care in time
Reclaiming yet thoughtless you enough
Times to be sure your truth
Shone bright, member of long ways discovered
As it was only ways
Possible here, now, complete.

Nerja, Costa Del Sol

The blind leading the blind
In an old port city
Famous for its skids
To the water front I go.
Hand in hand
With rejoicing and other
A grand slam it's not
Feeling a way that's best.
On Sea Wall with lemon
We have oysters over the water,
Tapas with wine,
Beautiful views.
Seeing's believing,
Believing in other,
You're too a leader
Today leading to the sea.

Shimmer Shimmer You All

True it is I juggled you
Daring too, we were, and so
Past is past, now I defer
You juggling past me, a star
Wished on, a grace relinquished
For what I'm not knowing
Bowing out. For you I wished
Perfection mixed with sunshine
Tears... rolling still this ball of love
Reflecting all within I shoved
My whole carcass upon above
Insides, that your juggling thrive.
Now with ease I breathe, you air
Thoughts so graceful I've no remiss
Balancing or juggling this
Us. We stand, we do deliver
Forever, a shimmering cure-all.

Take pie, get round to it
Slice by four, squarely view it,
Serve with no angles
Generous if you're with it,
Filling whole with what's left
Love for the going through it.

Kitty Cat Éclat

That smile on lips so familiar, good
Eyes twinkling where you stood the test
This time, clear, unbelieving, yet fine, giving
In I did, I do, I cannot believe...
I will deceive yet you are there
Bearing well, with patience
Perfect in that way you are, so
Sensibility having spoken, now
We arrive going separate ways
Knowing by means chosen we'll again
Home find being miraculous,
Miracle being our song's own home.
Chosen then that provender
Still will us again bear our loves.

old maple eulogy

(for a Greenlake Maple loved of neighbors, April 2012)

Beautiful, dutiful, full you are nymph
Of wood, when I see the rain in your
Hair, think I because it's there you feel
Well passed, our years in life together, we
In the middle of our tears landed in wood
Lands with no end, pleasing, staying,
Hearing me sing like wind stirring for
You that hair to shake free there the dew
Maple blessed by you for us forever
Lastly, blessing as you did my eyes for
Thought I so, and came to you
As dew comes to ground again
Gold you made it then, to dun,
So what begun seeming of pure chance
Ends at last as forests passing forever.

We did not need to go there
but there it was in wait,
a golden ringed doorway
with open hearts as bait.

Includes 3 titles:
European Divergininity
Beginners' Euphone
Macabre Gnome Dance [retitled]

By Claudia Link and Patrick King,
a look from the Puget Sound in
less than 100 pages.

SPECIAL THANKS TO FAMILY AND FRIENDS WHO CONTINUE TO HAVE GREAT PATIENCE IN THE FACE OF ANOTHER DAY.

www.ingramcontent.com/pod-product-compliance
Ingram Content Group UK Ltd.
Pitfield, Milton Keynes, MK11 3LW, UK
UKHW020220250726
13967UKWH00001B/100

9 781300 031772